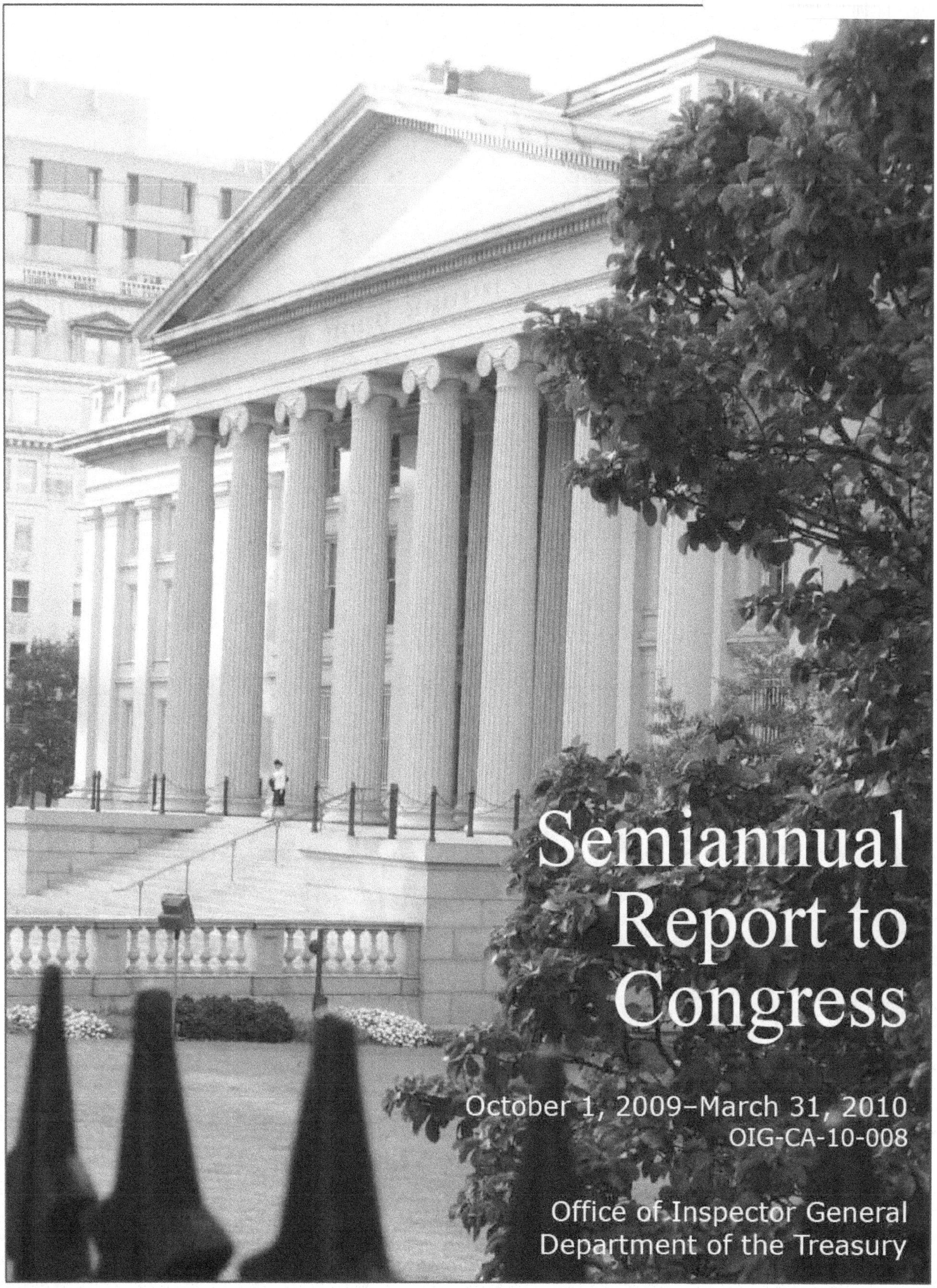

Semiannual Report to Congress

October 1, 2009–March 31, 2010
OIG-CA-10-008

Office of Inspector General
Department of the Treasury

Highlights

- During this semiannual reporting period, 40 audit products were issued.

- We completed material loss reviews of six failed Treasury-regulated financial institutions that together resulted in a loss to the Deposit Insurance Fund of $1.2 billion. High concentrations in certain types of loans (including high risk land and construction loans), ineffective management, exacerbated by the significant drops in real estate value were primary reasons for all of the institutions' failures.

- We issued two audit reports as part of our ongoing oversight of Treasury's more than $20 billion of non-Internal Revenue Service spending authority under the American Recovery and Reinvestment Act of 2009. The two reports issued during this period were part of the Recovery Accountability and Transparency Board-coordinated government-wide reviews. In the first review, we found that data prepared by Treasury regarding the adequacy of Recovery Act staffing levels, qualifications, and training were not reliable. Management immediately agreed to correct the problems with the survey data as well as address any issues identified once reliable data was obtained. In the second review, we found weaknesses in Treasury's processes for reviewing recipient data. Again, management was receptive to our recommendations for improvement.

- KPMG LLP, under our oversight, issued an unqualified opinion on the Department of the Treasury's fiscal year 2009 financial statements. The auditors reported two material weaknesses related to financial management practices at the Departmental level and financial systems and reporting at the Internal Revenue Service.

- Our office issued its fourth report on Suspicious Activity Report (SAR) data quality. SARs filed by financial institutions with the Financial Crimes Enforcement Network are critical to law enforcement efforts to combat, among other things, money laundering and terrorist financing. Three prior audits revealed that a large percentage of SARs contained missing or inaccurate data. Our latest audit concluded that SAR data quality had not significantly improved by 2006. We found that 59 percent of the approximately 1.1 million SARs filed in fiscal year 2006 contained omissions or incorrect, inconsistent, or inappropriate information in 1 or more of 17 critical fields. Management has since undertaken efforts to improve the quality and integrity of SAR data.

- Our Office of Investigations determined that the daughter of a deceased Metropolitan D.C. police officer unlawfully received $54,000 from a pension fund administered by the Department. The Department is in the process of reclaiming the funds.

- An OIG Special Agent received an award for his contributions to successful prosecutions in an identity theft case. Another Office of Investigations employee participated on a Treasury Team that was recognized for achieving significant energy savings.

Message From the Inspector General

Over the past 6 months, my office focused almost exclusively on performing material loss reviews of failed banks and thrifts regulated by the Office of the Comptroller of the Currency (OCC) and the Office of Thrift Supervision (OTS). These reviews are mandated by the Federal Deposit Insurance Act whenever a failed Treasury-regulated financial institution causes a loss of $25 million or more to the Federal Deposit Insurance Corporation's Deposit Insurance Fund. During the current economic crisis through March 31st of this year, my office has completed and issued 17 such reviews and has another 32 underway. The failures of these 49 Treasury-regulated financial institutions have cost the Deposit Insurance Fund an estimated $34 billion.

The results of these reviews have provided a great deal of information as to why these institutions failed, as well as to the quality of supervision exercised by OCC and OTS. Several broad themes have emerged with regard to both. Clearly, the severity and swiftness of the recession and, in particular, the decline in the real estate market were factors in the failure of most of these institutions. However, that does not tell the whole story. We have found that time and again many of these failed institutions offered risky loan products and engaged in poor underwriting practices as they embarked on strategies of rapid growth--growth often funded by volatile funding sources. The risks presented by poor underwriting were often magnified by high concentrations in one particular type of loan product, geographic location, or both. In addition, the management and boards of these institutions were often ineffective in monitoring their risks and failed to correct regulator-identified problems.

On the supervision side, for the most part we found that through its examinations, the regulators were identifying and reporting the unsafe and unsound practices that the institutions engaged in, sometimes as far back as 2003 and 2004. What we are, and have been, most critical of is the absence of timely and forceful enforcement action when it may have made a difference. We also frequently questioned the high ratings given to these institutions (known as CAMELS ratings) right up until shortly before the institutions failed, especially when considering the repetitive nature of many of problems identified in the bank examinations. Too much reliance was placed on the ability and willingness of bank management to fix their problems through "moral suasion." Furthermore, in rating the institutions, we believe that the examiners often gave too much weight to the fact that the institutions were profitable and their loans were performing and not enough to the magnitude of risks that these institutions had taken on. In the end, the profits and loan performance were elusive.

Based on our completed reviews, we have made numerous recommendations to both OCC and OTS to improve their respective bank examination processes. Both have been very responsive to our recommendations and in many instances have already implemented corrective actions to address them.

The Administration and Congress are currently working on a variety of sweeping changes to the financial regulatory environment. Certainly the current financial crisis has revealed gaps in financial regulation that need to be addressed, such as oversight of investment banks, regulation of derivatives, and policy implications of "too big to fail." However, our work has shown that for regulating the safety and soundness of federally insured depository institutions, OCC and OTS had examination processes in place that were able to identify problems early on and many tools available to prevent banks and thrifts from continuing to take on levels of risk that could drive them into failure. This is not to say that the examiners have all the tools they need, as oftentimes they are impeded by the fact that supervisory guidance can be challenged because it is not a law or regulation. Recently, Comptroller Dugan in addressing a group of community bankers stated that there was a "need to revisit the issue of the appropriate regulatory response to CRE [commercial real estate] lending concentrations, especially for construction and development lending and especially for concentrations supported by noncore funding." This is an acknowledgement of one problem area that we have found in our post mortems of failed institutions and a recognition that the regulators need to do more.

Regardless of the changes that result from the Administration's and Congress' efforts to reform the financial regulatory environment, the challenge for Treasury and its bank regulators will be to take the lessons learned from the current wave of failed institutions and ensure that they do not miss this opportunity to make fundamental and lasting changes to their supervisory approach going forward. Our challenge will be to provide the oversight and forward looking audit work that can help the Department and our Nation in these efforts.

Eric M. Thorson
Inspector General

Contents

Overview of the Office of Inspector General

The Department of the Treasury's Office of Inspector General (OIG) was established pursuant to the 1988 amendment to the Inspector General Act of 1978. OIG is headed by an Inspector General appointed by the President, with the advice and consent of the Senate. Serving with the Inspector General in the immediate office is a Deputy Inspector General. OIG performs independent, objective reviews of Treasury programs and operations, except for those of the Internal Revenue Service (IRS) and the Troubled Asset Relief Program (TARP), and keeps the Secretary of the Treasury and Congress fully informed of problems, deficiencies, and the need for corrective action. The Treasury Inspector General for Tax Administration performs oversight related to IRS. A special inspector general and the Government Accountability Office (GAO) perform oversight related to TARP.

OIG is organized into four divisions: (1) Office of Audit, (2) Office of Investigations, (3) Office of Counsel, and (4) Office of Management. OIG is headquartered in Washington, DC, and has an audit office in Boston, Massachusetts.

The Office of Audit performs and supervises audits, attestation engagements, and evaluations. The Assistant Inspector General for Audit has two deputies. One is primarily responsible for performance audits, and the other is primarily responsible for financial management, information technology, and financial assistance audits.

The Office of Investigations, under the leadership of the Assistant Inspector General for Investigations, performs investigations and conducts initiatives to detect and prevent fraud, waste, and abuse in Treasury programs and operations under our jurisdiction. The Office of Investigations also performs integrity oversight reviews of select Treasury bureaus.

The Office of Counsel (1) processes all Freedom of Information Act/Privacy Act requests and administrative appeals on behalf of OIG; (2) processes all discovery requests for information held by OIG; (3) represents OIG in administrative Equal Employment Opportunity and Merit Systems Protection Board proceedings; (4) conducts ethics training and provides ethics advice to OIG employees and ensures OIG compliance with financial disclosure requirements; (5) reviews proposed legislation and regulations relating to the Department; (6) reviews administrative subpoenas; (7) reviews and responds to all *Gigolo* requests for information about Treasury personnel who may testify in trials; and (8) provides legal advice to the other OIG divisions.

The Office of Management provides services to maintain the OIG administrative infrastructure. It also manages the Treasury OIG Hotline to facilitate reporting of allegations involving Treasury programs and activities. The Assistant Inspector General for Management oversees these functions.

As of March 31, 2010, OIG had 146 full-time staff. OIG's fiscal year 2010 appropriation was $29.7 million.

Treasury Management and Performance Challenges

In accordance with the Reports Consolidation Act of 2000, the Treasury Inspector General annually provides the Secretary of the Treasury with his perspective on the most serious management and performance challenges facing the Department. The Secretary includes these challenges in Treasury's annual agency financial report. In a memorandum to Secretary Geithner dated October 29, 2009, Inspector General Thorson reported one new challenge—management of American Recovery and Reinvestment Act (Recovery Act) programs—and four challenges from last year. Two previously reported challenges were removed. The following is an abridged description of the challenges reported and removed.

Management of Treasury's New Authorities Related to Distressed Financial Markets (Repeat Challenge)

Treasury, along with the Federal Reserve, the Federal Deposit Insurance Corporation (FDIC), and the Federal Housing Finance Agency, has taken unprecedented actions to address the current financial crisis. To assist in those efforts, Congress passed the Housing and Economic Recovery Act in July 2008, which gave Treasury broad new authorities to address the distressed financial condition of Fannie Mae and Freddie Mac. Less than 6 weeks later, the Federal Housing Finance Agency put both entities into conservatorship.

As the turmoil in the financial markets increased, Treasury sought and obtained additional authorities through passage of the Emergency Economic Stabilization Act (EESA)

in October 2008. EESA, commonly known as TARP, gave the Treasury Secretary $700 billion to, among other things, (1) purchase capital in qualifying U.S.-controlled financial institutions and (2) buy, maintain, and sell toxic mortgage-related assets from financial institutions.

After EESA was enacted, the Department aggressively moved forward to loosen the credit market by purchasing senior preferred stock in nine of the nation's largest financial institutions. Since then, hundreds of other financial institutions have also participated in the Capital Purchase Program (CPP).

EESA established a special inspector general for TARP and imposed oversight and periodic reporting requirements on both the special inspector general and GAO. GAO has reported that TARP in general and CPP in particular, along with other efforts by the Federal Reserve and FDIC, had made important contributions to help stabilize credit markets. However, GAO also reported that many challenges and uncertainties remain. GAO further noted that other programs, such as the Public-Private Investment Program and the Home Affordable Modification Program, still face implementation and operational challenges.

As conditions improve, Treasury will need to work with its partners to disassemble the structure established to support recovery efforts and ensure that federal funds no longer needed for those efforts are returned in an orderly manner to the Treasury general fund.

Regulation of National Banks and Thrifts (Repeat Challenge)

Although many factors have contributed to the turmoil in the financial markets, Treasury's

Office of the Comptroller of the Currency (OCC) and Office of Thrift Supervision (OTS) did not force timely correction of unsafe and unsound practices by failed institutions under their supervision.

Both OCC and OTS have been responsive to our recommendations for improving supervision. It is essential; however, that OCC and OTS continue to take a critical look at their supervisory processes to identify why those processes did not prevent or mitigate the practices that led to the current crisis and what can be done to better protect the financial health of the banking industry and consumers going forward.

Recognizing that the focus of EESA and the Recovery Act is on the current crisis, another consideration is the need to identify, monitor, and manage emerging domestic and global systemic economic risks. Moreover, these emerging risks may go beyond the current U.S. regulatory structure. Treasury and its regulatory partners must continue to diligently monitor both regulated and unregulated products and markets for new systemic risks that may require action.

Finally, both the administration and Congress are considering proposals for regulatory reform. Treasury, OCC, and OTS will need to work in concert with the other affected federal bank regulators to ensure a smooth and effective transition to the new regulatory structure that emerges.

Management of Recovery Act Programs (New Challenge)

Treasury is responsible for overseeing an estimated $150 billion of Recovery Act funding

and tax relief. Treasury's oversight responsibilities include grants for specified energy property in lieu of tax credits, grants to states for low-income housing projects in lieu of tax credits, increased Community Development Financial Institutions (CDFI) Fund grants and tax credits, economic recovery payments to social security beneficiaries and others, and payments to U.S. territories for distribution to their citizens. Many of these programs are new to Treasury and involve very large dollar amounts. As a result, Treasury faces immense challenges in ensuring that the programs achieve their intended purposes, provide for accountability and transparency, and are free from fraud and abuse.

Treasury's Recovery Act grants in lieu of tax credit programs—for specified energy property and to states for low-income housing projects— are estimated to cost almost $20 billion over their lives. Treasury has dedicated only a small number of staff to award and monitor these funds. We have concerns that the current staffing level is not commensurate with the size of these programs.

The Deputy Secretary and the Senior Accountable Official have shown a strong commitment to implementing an effective control structure over Recovery Act activities and strong support for our oversight effort.

Management of Capital Investments (Repeat Challenge)

Managing large capital investments, particularly information technology investments, is a difficult challenge for any organization, whether public or private. In prior years, we have reported on a number of capital investment projects that either failed or had serious problems. Treasury is now making the transition to a new, mission-critical telecommunications system, TNet. The overall value of the TNet contract is estimated at $270 million. The transition, however, is now late. Treasury must exercise continuous vigilance in managing its capital investments.

Anti-Money Laundering and Terrorist Financing/Bank Secrecy Act Enforcement (Repeat Challenge)

Treasury faces unique challenges in carrying out its responsibilities under the Bank Secrecy Act (BSA) and USA Patriot Act to prevent and detect money laundering and terrorist financing. Although the Financial Crimes Enforcement Network (FinCEN) is responsible for administering BSA, a large number of other federal and state entities participate in efforts to ensure compliance with BSA. Many of these entities also participate in efforts to ensure compliance with U.S. foreign sanction programs administered by Treasury's Office of Foreign Assets Control (OFAC).

FinCEN and OFAC have entered into memoranda of understanding with many federal and state regulators in an attempt to build a consistent and effective process. However, these instruments are nonbinding and carry no penalties for violations.

Although BSA reports are critical to law enforcement, past audits have shown that many contain incomplete or erroneous data and that examination coverage by financial institution regulators of BSA compliance has been limited.

Given the criticality of this management challenge to the Department's mission, we continue to consider BSA and OFAC programs

as inherently high-risk. Adding to this risk in the current environment is the risk that financial institutions and their regulators may decrease their attention to BSA and OFAC program compliance as they address safety and soundness concerns.

Challenges Removed

We removed corporate management as an overarching management challenge, first identified as a challenge in 2004, because the Department has made significant progress in building up a sustainable corporate control structure. We also removed information security as a management and performance challenge, first identified in 2001, because Treasury has made significant strides in improving and institutionalizing its information security controls.

Significant Audits and Evaluations

Financial Management

Financial Audits

Consolidated Financial Statements

KPMG LLP, an independent public accountant, working under our supervision, issued an unqualified opinion on the Department's fiscal years 2009 and 2008 consolidated financial statements. The audit identified significant deficiencies related to (1) financial management practices at the departmental level, (2) financial systems and reporting at IRS, (3) financial accounting and reporting at the Office of Financial Stability, and (4) information system controls at the Financial Management Service (FMS). The significant deficiencies related to financial management practices at the departmental level and financial systems and reporting at IRS are considered material weaknesses. KPMG also reported that the Department's financial management systems are not in substantial compliance with the Federal Financial Management Improvement Act of 1996.

In addition, the audit identified a reportable instance of noncompliance with laws and regulations related to section 6325[1] of the Internal Revenue Code. **(OIG-10-023)**

---

[1] The internal revenue code grants the IRS the power to file a lien against the property of any taxpayer who neglects or refuses to pay all assessed federal taxes. Under the internal revenue code section 6325, the IRS is required to release a federal tax lien within 30 days after the date the tax liability is satisfied, or has become legally unenforceable, or the Secretary of the Treasury has accepted a bond for the assessed tax.

In connection with its audit of Treasury's consolidated financial statements, KPMG issued a management letter that identified other matters involving internal control and Treasury operations related to (1) financial reporting standards for Treasury's component entities, (2) opening balances, (3) intragovernmental transactions and activities, (4) reconciliation of the statement of budgetary resources to budget reports, (5) review of audit logs for the database that supports the Treasury Information Executive Repository (TIER), (6) documentation of baseline configurations for the production servers that support TIER and CFO Vision in the system security plan, and (7) encryption of user sessions with TIER and CFO Vision. These matters were identified during the audit but were not required to be included in the auditor's report. **(OIG-10-035)**

Other Financial Audits

The Chief Financial Officers Act of 1990, as amended by the Government Management Reform Act of 1994, requires annual financial statement audits of Treasury and Office of Management and Budget (OMB) designated entities. OMB has designated IRS for annual financial statement audits. The financial statements of certain other Treasury component entities are audited pursuant to other requirements or due to their materiality to Treasury's consolidated financial statements.

The following table shows audit results for fiscal years 2009 and 2008.

Treasury-audited financial statements and related audits						
Entity	Fiscal year 2009 audit results			Fiscal year 2008 audit results		
	Opinion	Material weaknesses	Other significant deficiencies	Opinion	Material weaknesses	Other significant deficiencies
Government Management Reform Act/Chief Financial Officers Act requirements						
Department of the Treasury	UQ	2	2	UQ	1	2
Internal Revenue Service (A)	UQ	2	0	UQ	3	1
Other required audits						
Department of the Treasury's Special-Purpose Financial Statements	Q	1	0	UQ	0	1
Office of Financial Stability (TARP) (A)	UQ	0	2	N/A	(D)	N/A
Bureau of Engraving and Printing	UQ	0	0	UQ	0	0
Community Development Financial Institutions Fund (B)	UQ	0	3	UQ	0	2
Office of DC Pensions	UQ	0	0	UQ	0	0
Exchange Stabilization Fund	UQ	0	1	UQ	1	1
Federal Financing Bank	UQ	0	0	UQ	0	0
Office of the Comptroller of the Currency	UQ	0	0	UQ	0	0
Office of Thrift Supervision	UQ	0	0	UQ	0	0
Treasury Forfeiture Fund	UQ	0	0	UQ	0	0
Mint						
Financial statements	UQ	0	0	UQ	0	2
Custodial gold and silver reserves	UQ	0	0	UQ	0	0
Other audited accounts that are material to Treasury financial statements						
Bureau of the Public Debt						
Schedule of Federal Debt (A)	UQ	0	0	UQ	0	0
Government trust funds	UQ	0	0	UQ	0	1
Financial Management Service						
Treasury-managed accounts	UQ	0	1	UQ	0	1
Operating cash of the federal government	UQ	0	1	UQ	0	0
Management-initiated audit						
FinCEN	UQ	0	0	UQ	0	0
Alcohol and Tobacco Tax and Trade Bureau	C	C	C	N/A	N/A	N/A
UQ	Unqualified opinion					
Q	Qualified opinion due to omission of a required disclosure and misstatement of certain account balances in the financial statement notes					
(A)	Audited by GAO					
(B)	Full-scope audit of financial statements for fiscal year 2009, audit of the Statement of Financial Position only for fiscal year 2008					
(C)	Audit report not issued as of March 31, 2010. Audit of Balance Sheet only for fiscal year 2009					
(D)	Entity was not audited before fiscal year 2009					
N/A	Entity was not audited					

The fiscal year 2009 audits of Treasury's component entities and its special-purpose financial statements identified the following material weakness and other significant deficiencies. These audits were performed by KPMG or other independent public accountants under our supervision.

Material Weakness

- The Department's insufficient staffing resources, accounting processes, and related controls for the preparation of its special-purpose financial statements. **(OIG-10-029)**

Other Significant Deficiencies

- The CDFI Fund's controls over (1) the accounting process for estimating loan loss reserves, (2) accounting for investments, and (3) the preparation and review of the financial statements. **(OIG-10-009)**

- The Exchange Stabilization Fund's controls over financial reporting and technical accounting and monitoring of foreign currency transactions. **(OIG-10-027)**

- The FMS information technology controls over systems managed by FMS and third parties. **(OIG-10-018, OIG-10-019)**

The auditors also issued management letters that identified other matters that were not required to be included in the reports on the fiscal year 2009 audits of the financial statements of the Bureau of Engraving and Printing (BEP) **(OIG-10-006)**, CDFI Fund **(OIG-10-010)**, Office of D.C. Pensions **(OIG-10-016)**, Exchange Stabilization Fund **(OIG-10-028)**, Federal Financing Bank **(OIG-10-008)**, Mint **(OIG-10-014)**, OCC **(OIG-10-025)**, and OTS **(OIG-10-032)** and the fiscal year 2009 audit of the FMS Schedule of Non-Entity Government-wide Cash **(OIG-10-021)**. In addition, the auditors issued two sensitive-but-unclassified management reports that detailed FMS's significant deficiency related to information technology controls over systems managed by FMS and third parties and recommended corrective actions. **(OIG-10-020, OIG-10-022)**.

The following instances of noncompliance with the Federal Financial Management Improvement Act, which all relate to IRS, were reported in connection with the audit of the Department's fiscal year 2009 consolidated financial statements.

Condition	Type of noncompliance
Core general ledger system does not conform to Federal Financial Management System Requirements contained in OMB Circular.A-127, Financial Management Systems. (first reported in fiscal year 1997)	Federal financial management systems requirements
Material weaknesses in internal control over information security continue to threaten (1) integrity of the financial statements and the accuracy and availability of financial information needed to support day-to-day decision making and (2) confidentiality of proprietary information. (first reported in fiscal year 1997)	Federal financial management systems requirements
Automated systems for tax-related transactions did not support the net taxes receivable amount on the balance sheet and other required supplemental information related to uncollected taxes–compliance assessments and write-offs–in accordance with Statement of Federal Financial Accounting Standards No. 7, Accounting for Revenue and Other Financing Sources and Concepts for Reconciling Budgetary and Financial Accounting. (first reported in fiscal year 1997)	Federal accounting standards
IRS's core general ledger system for tax-related activities does not comply with the U.S. Government Standard General Ledger at the transaction level and also does not post transactions in conformance with Standard General Ledger posting models. (first reported in fiscal year 1997)	U.S. Government Standard General Ledger

The status of these noncompliances, including progress in implementing remediation plans, will be evaluated as part of the audit of Treasury's fiscal year 2010 financial statements.

Attestation Engagement

KPMG LLP, working under our supervision, issued an unqualified opinion that the Bureau of the Public Debt (BPD) Trust Fund Management Branch's assertions pertaining to the schedule of assets and liabilities and related schedule of activity of selected trust funds, as of and for the year ended September 30, 2009, are fairly stated. These schedules relate to the functions of the Trust Fund Management Branch as custodian of the Federal Supplementary Medical Insurance Trust Fund, Federal Hospital Insurance Trust Fund, Highway Trust Fund, Airport and Airway Trust Fund, Hazardous Substance Superfund Trust Fund, Leaking Underground Storage Tank Trust Fund, Oil Spill Liability Trust Fund, Harbor Maintenance Trust Fund, Inland Waterways Trust Fund, and South Dakota Terrestrial Wildlife Habitat Restoration Trust

Fund. The attestation examination did not identify any significant deficiencies in internal control or instances of reportable noncompliance with laws and regulations. **(OIG-10-005)**

Information Technology

Federal Information Security Management Act Evaluation of Treasury for Fiscal Year 2009

The Federal Information Security Management Act of 2002 (FISMA) requires our office to perform an annual, independent evaluation of Treasury's information security program and practices. We contracted with KPMG to perform, under our supervision, the evaluation of FISMA compliance for the Department's unclassified, non-IRS systems. TIGTA performed the annual evaluation for IRS. Based on the results reported by KPMG and TIGTA, we determined that Treasury's information security program was in place and was generally consistent with FISMA.

However, the evaluation of Treasury's unclassified non-IRS systems indicated that additional steps are required to ensure that Treasury's information security risk management program and practices fully comply with applicable National Institute of Standards and Technology standards and guidelines and FISMA requirements. Specifically, (1) minimum security control baselines were not sufficiently tested or implemented (repeat finding); (2) the breach notification policy required by OMB had not been finalized and issued (repeat finding); (3) the Departmental Offices Federal Desktop Core Configuration image was not fully implemented (repeat finding); (4) BPD was not using a Security Content Automation Protocol validated tool; (5) FMS's Plan of Action and Milestone was not consistently updated in accordance with bureau policy; (6) the frequency of vulnerability assessment scanning at BPD was not in line with bureau and Treasury policy; and (7) an E-authentication risk assessment was not performed at FinCEN. TIGTA reported that IRS had made steady progress in complying with FISMA requirements. TIGTA also found significant improvements in IRS information technology contingency plan testing and additional improvements in annual security controls testing, which were identified as areas needing improvement in its 2008 FISMA evaluation. TIGTA noted that IRS still needs to take action in the areas of certification and accreditation, and configuration management. **(OIG-CA-10-003)**

CDFI Fund's Access Controls and Configuration Management

We determined that the CDFI Fund has sufficient protection in place for its network and systems. Specifically, most CDFI Fund systems were up to date with the latest patches. Also, CDFI Fund staff had implemented a suite of monitoring tools for its network that reported current patch levels, monitored for suspicious activities, and provided notification to administrators of potentially suspicious activities. However, we noted that improvements are needed in key access controls and in configuration management to prevent unauthorized users from gaining access and compromising data on the CDFI Fund's public web site and within its network. We found that (1) weak passwords were used in CDFI Fund applications and systems, (2) CDFI Fund systems were configured with insecure default settings, and (3) a critical patch was not applied for one CDFI Fund system. In a written response, the CDFI Fund Director provided plans for corrective actions that were responsive to our seven recommendations addressing these findings. **(OIG-10-037)**

Programs and Operations

Bank Failures and Material Loss Reviews

OCC and OTS regulate and supervise many of the Nation's banks and thrifts. Specifically, OCC regulates national chartered banks and OTS regulates thrifts.

In 1991, Congress enacted the Federal Deposit Insurance Corporation Improvement Act (FDICIA) amending the Federal Deposit Insurance Act following the failures of about 1,000 banks and thrifts between 1986 and 1990 that resulted in billions in losses to the Deposit Insurance Fund. The amendments require the banking regulators take specified supervisory actions when they identify unsafe or unsound practices or conditions.

Section 38(k) of FDICIA requires that the cognizant inspector general for the primary federal regulator review the failure of a financial institution when the estimated loss to the Deposit Insurance Fund becomes material (defined as a loss that exceeds the greater of $25 million or 2 percent of the institution's total assets). As part of the material loss review (MLR), we determine the causes of the failure and assess the supervision over the institution, including the implementation of the Prompt Corrective Action (PCA) provisions in FDICIA.[2] As appropriate, we also make recommendations for preventing any such loss in the future.

Since the current economic crisis began in 2007 through March 31, 2010, FDIC and other regulators have closed 208 banks and thrifts. Sixty-five (65) of these institutions were regulated by Treasury. Sixteen (16) of these institutions did not require an MLR to be performed as the loss to the Deposit Insurance Fund was not material. In prior semiannual reports, we reported on 11 MLRs completed during the current crisis. This semi-annual reporting period we completed 6 MLRs , 4

supervised by OCC and 2 supervised by OTS. These MLRs are described in more detail below. As of the end of the reporting period, we had 32 MLRs in progress, and we expect additional bank and thrift failures in the coming months.

From the 17 MLRs completed in total during current economic crisis, we have seen a number of trends emerge. With respect to the causes of institutions' failures, we found overly aggressive growth strategies fueled by volatile and costly wholesale funding (e.g., brokered deposits, Federal Home Loan Bank loans, etc.); risky lending products such as option adjustable rate mortgages; unsound underwriting; high asset concentrations to include high concentrations in commercial real estate loans; and inadequate risk management systems. In addition, the management and boards of these institutions were often not effective in monitoring and managing their risks. The economic recession and in particular the decline in the real estate market was also a major factor in most failures.

With respect to OCC's and OTS's supervision, we found that the regulators conducted regular and timely examinations and identified operational problems, but were slow to take timely and aggressive enforcement action. We also found that in rating these institutions, examiners gave too much weight to the fact that the institutions were profitable and their loans were performing and not enough weight given to the amount of risk that these institutions had taken on. We also noted that regulators took the appropriate PCA actions when warranted but those actions did not save the institutions. While it is too soon to comment on the effectiveness of the PCA provisions of FDICIA more generally, this is an area we believe needs to be examined further.

---

[2] PCA is a framework of supervisory actions, set forth in law, for insured institutions that are not adequately capitalized. It was intended to ensure that action is taken when an institution becomes financially troubled in order to prevent a failure or minimize resulting losses. These actions become increasingly severe as the institution falls into lower capital categories. The capital categories are well-capitalized, adequately capitalized, undercapitalized, significantly undercapitalized, and critically undercapitalized.

OCC-Regulated Institutions Reviewed

Silverton Bank, N.A. of Atlanta, Georgia (closed May 1, 2009; estimated loss to the Deposit Insurance Fund, $608.3 million)

The primary cause of Silverton's failure was an excessive concentration in commercial real estate (CRE) loans. Deficient credit risk management processes, combined with the rapid decline in the economic environment, resulted in the deterioration of Silverton's asset quality, including a substantial volume of problem loans and significant loan losses. These loan losses, along with the high cost of funding, significantly diminished earnings and capital, impairing Silverton's ability to successfully implement and sustain its business strategy.

OCC approved Silverton's conversion from a state-chartered bank to a nationally chartered bank in August 2007 despite significant weaknesses identified by OCC examiners during a preconversion examination and the declining housing market. We believe that OCC should not have approved Silverton's conversion in August 2007 and instead should have deferred approval until those weaknesses had been addressed.

Subsequent to the bank's conversion, we believe that OCC could not have done anything significantly different to prevent Silverton's failure and the material loss to the Deposit Insurance Fund. That said, there was a serious lapse in OCC's supervision of Silverton shortly after its conversion and swifter action might have reduced the bank's aggressive growth and amount of loss to the Deposit Insurance Fund. Specifically, an examiner-in-charge was not immediately assigned to Silverton. Furthermore a 17 month gap existed between completion of the last joint full-scope examination of the bank

by its prior regulator and the start of the first full-scope examination by OCC.

During our MLR, OCC completed an internal lessons-learned review of the Silverton failure. That review also concluded that the decision to approve the conversion was flawed. Among other things, the reviewers recommended that OCC consider a quality assurance review process over charter conversions. In subsequent discussions, OCC officials stated that performing second-level reviews of charter conversions prior to approval would be a better approach than an after-the-fact quality assurance review. Such a process, however, had not yet been formalized in OCC policies and procedures.

At the time our report was issued, OCC was in the process of planning and taking steps to address our recommendations that OCC (1) promptly assign an examiner-in-charge and ensure continuous supervisory coverage of converted institutions, (2) determine that banks seeking conversion to a national charter satisfactorily address significant deficiencies identified by OCC or prior regulators before approval, and (3) formalize the process for second-level reviews of charter conversions. **(OIG-10-033)**

Omni National Bank of Atlanta, Georgia (closed March 27, 2009; estimated loss to the Deposit Insurance Fund, $288.2 million)

Omni failed because of significant losses in CRE loans. The bank grew rapidly from 2003 through 2008, in large part from its increased number of CRE loans. The bank's board of directors and management failed to adequately control concentration risk or ensure that adequate internal controls over lending were implemented. Omni's lack of controls led to deficient underwriting, credit administration, and appraisal practices. The bank's most problematic CRE loans were short-term redevelopment loans originated by its Community Development Lending Division. The bank's underwriting of redevelopment loans relied extensively on anticipated appreciation in property values and far less on borrowers' creditworthiness or ability to repay obligations. The bank's deficiencies were exacerbated by the decline in the real estate and secondary loan markets. These declines made it necessary for Omni to foreclose on a high volume of overvalued properties and recognize significant losses when borrowers could not sell properties to repay their obligations. The Community Development Lending Division also engaged in questionable lending practices, which were under investigation by OCC at the time of our MLR. We also referred these matters to the Treasury Inspector General's Office of Investigations.

OCC's supervision of Omni was inadequate and likely led to greater losses to the Deposit Insurance Fund. Although OCC performed timely full-scope examinations of the bank, it was not until the examination began in January 2008 that OCC fully identified Omni's lack of management controls and oversight, uncontrolled asset growth, and high-risk unsafe and unsound lending practices. The conditions cited in the report for this examination resulted in OCC's downgrading the bank's CAMELS composite rating from 2 to 5 and implementing formal enforcement action. These deficiencies, however, had existed at the bank for several years and were not identified in prior examinations.

We also identified two other matters that negatively affected OCC's supervision of Omni. In 2007, a time period critical to the decline of

the bank, OCC failed to perform quarterly monitoring activities. As a result, OCC was unaware of the deterioration of the bank's condition until its January 2008 full-scope examination. OCC also had not established a formal policy for rotating examiners-in-charge of midsize and community banks. At Omni, the same examiner-in-charge was in place during four consecutive examination cycles, from 2003 through 2007. During those cycles, few problems were identified, and the problems that were noted were not fully corrected. OCC acknowledged that many of the deficiencies cited in the report for the examination that began in January 2008 had existed in prior years but had not previously been identified as problems.

OCC acted forcefully against the bank in 2008 when it appropriately used its PCA authority. Because of reporting irregularities, OCC required the bank to re-file its December 31, 2007, call report. The updated call report disclosed that the bank was at the adequately capitalized level as of December 31, 2007, and would have been prohibited from accepting some of the $120 million in brokered deposits it had acquired during the first 6 months of 2008. Omni's ability to obtain these brokered deposits may have increased the loss to the Deposit Insurance Fund.

We also reported that OCC took formal action against Omni but that action took nearly 9 months. Specifically, in February 2008, OCC examiners informed Omni that the bank's condition warranted a downgrade and formal enforcement action. OCC, however, did not implement a consent order until October 2008. OCC officials cited the following reasons for the length of time it took to implement the consent order: (1) there was no immediate need to stop unsafe and unsound practices since the bank had ceased redevelopment lending and other deficient lending practices and (2) to take formal enforcement action, OCC must be able to introduce into evidence sufficient findings and legal support—the report of examination is typically used to document the findings and legal support, and was issued in September 2008 with the consent order following within 3 weeks. While we acknowledged OCC's need to develop sufficient support for an enforcement action, we believe the supervisory process used to issue the Omni consent order was slow and pointed to a need for OCC to reassess its process.

We recommended that OCC (1) review processes to ensure that more timely enforcement action is taken once the need for such action is identified; (2) impress upon examiner staff the importance of completing all activities in annual supervisory cycles, including quarterly monitoring, and ensure that supervisors see that quarterly monitoring activities are scheduled and carried out; and (3) implement a policy for examiner-in-charge rotation for midsize and community banks.

OCC agreed that there were shortcomings in its supervision of Omni but maintained that the timing of the October 2008 consent order was in compliance with its policy. OCC also agreed that periodic monitoring is integral to effective supervision and stated it would continue to reinforce this expectation to examining staff. OCC also agreed that there is a benefit to formalizing a rotation policy for midsize and community banks and stated that it was developing such a policy. While we believe timely enforcement action was needed, we accept OCC's assertion that current policies are sufficient and consider our recommendation concerning the timeliness of enforcement action to be closed. OCC's completed and planned

actions regarding periodic monitoring and the rotation of examiners-in-charge were responsive to our recommendations. **(OIG-10-017)**

TeamBank, National Association of Paola, Kansas (closed March 20, 2009; estimated loss to the Deposit Insurance Fund, $98.4 million)

TeamBank failed primarily because its board and management did not provide effective oversight and establish adequate controls before embarking on a high-risk growth strategy with a concentration in CRE loans, as well as its deficient underwriting and credit administration and heavy reliance on non-core funding. In fact, the chief executive officer/president dominated the lending function as TeamBank's de facto chief credit officer. A decline in the real estate market exacerbated these conditions.

OCC's supervision did not adequately address TeamBank's problems to prevent a material loss to the Deposit Insurance Fund. OCC did not raise significant issues to the level of matters requiring attention (these are items noted by the examiner during an examination that deviate from sound governance, internal control, and risk management principles, which may adversely affect the bank's earnings or capital, risk profile, or reputation if not addressed) in the 2006 examination. In addition, OCC examiners did not identify that TeamBank was being controlled by a chief executive officer/president with too much responsibility to manage the bank's risk profile and growth strategy until 2008. Furthermore, OCC did not review TeamBank's incentive compensation or bonus plans nor ensure that TeamBank conducted stress testing. The bank's credit administration and loan supervision practices, the level of classified assets, and a number of risk management issues should have been addressed in 2007 by examiners. We also concluded that OCC appropriately used its PCA authority as TeamBank's capital ratio fell to undercapitalized.

OCC concurred with our recommendation to emphasize to examiners the need to properly use matters requiring attention for supervisory concerns, adequately assess the responsibilities of a controlling official within a bank, review incentive compensation and bonus plans, and ensure that banks conduct transactional and portfolio stress testing when appropriate. **(OIG-10-001)**

Citizens National Bank of Macomb, Illinois (closed May 22, 2009; estimated loss to the Deposit Insurance Fund, $26 million)

Citizens National Bank (CNB) failed because management undertook a high-risk strategy of investing heavily in private-label collateralized mortgage obligations (CMO) and CRE loan participations funded principally with brokered deposits. This strategy led to rapid growth and high concentrations in CMOs and CRE loan participations. CNB's management and board did not establish controls commensurate with the risks associated with these assets. Significant portions of the CMOs and CRE loan participations subsequently went into default and were written off, causing the bank to become undercapitalized. There were also certain transactions related to the bank that are under further OCC review.

We believe that OCC could not have done anything significantly different to prevent CNB's failure and the material loss to the Deposit Insurance Fund. As CNB's capital levels fell, OCC also took appropriate actions under its PCA authority.

As a byproduct of its supervision over CNB, OCC had extensive internal discussions and worked with other supervisory agencies to provide proper guidance to the bank on risk-weighting of the downgraded CMOs. Subsequently, OCC issued additional guidance for risk management of structured investment securities.

As a regulatory matter, current law and regulatory standards permit banks to purchase investment grade CMOs without any statutory limitation. Given the experience with CNB and the National Bank of Commerce, which failed due to significant losses from preferred stock holdings in the Federal National Mortgage Association and the Federal Home Loan Mortgage Corporation, we believe that circumstances and conditions point to a potentially vulnerable regulatory area.[3]

We recommended that OCC (1) assess the adequacy of guidance on risk management of structured investment securities after it has been in use for a reasonable time and (2) work with its regulatory partners to determine whether to propose legislation or change regulatory guidance to establish limits or other controls for bank investments.

In response to the first recommendation, OCC agreed that it is important to have an ongoing process to assess the adequacy of its bank supervision policies. In this regard, its policy experts respond to questions from bankers and examiners regarding policy implementation. The interaction enables them to recognize situations where clarifications or additional guidance are needed. Also, in response to the second

---

[3] OIG, *Safety and Soundness: Material Loss Review of National Bank of Commerce* (OIG-09-042; issued Aug. 6, 2009).

recommendation, OCC stated that it is too early to say whether the final outcome of the deliberations with its regulatory partners will include changes in bank investment limits or risk management expectations. It will continue to study the situation and work with its regulatory partners when appropriate.

We consider the actions taken and planned by OCC responsive to the recommendations. We plan to evaluate OCC's process for updating guidance in the future. We will also monitor the progress of the interagency deliberations with respect to bank investment limits or risk management expectations as part of our future planned work. **(OIG-10-038)**

OTS-Regulated Institutions Reviewed

First Bank of Idaho, Ketchum, Idaho (closed; April 24, 2009; estimated loss to the Deposit Insurance Fund, $174.6 million)

First Bank of Idaho failed primarily because of (1) significant loan delinquencies and losses incurred on construction and land loans and (2) inadequate capital relative to the risk levels of its loans. These loans were concentrated in resort areas that experienced severe declines when the real estate market deteriorated. Starting in 2008, First Bank of Idaho relied on brokered deposits and federal borrowings due to its unstable funding structure, which included an unusually high amount of uninsured deposits. As the condition of the thrift deteriorated, First Bank of Idaho faced restrictions on its acceptance of brokered deposits, and limited access to federal borrowings. The losses in high-risk loans combined with the thrift's inability to obtain reliable funding created a liquidity crisis that prompted OTS to close the thrift.

OTS's supervision of First Bank of Idaho did not prevent a material loss to the Deposit Insurance Fund. OTS identified credit concentrations early on at the thrift but did not adequately address the risk associated with them. OTS took enforcement action against the thrift only after the concentrations became problematic. In addition, OTS reached supervisory judgments on two matters in 2006 that were inconsistent with First Bank of Idaho's rising risk profile. First, OTS did not take exception to the thrift's lowering of its target risk-based capital ratio from 11 percent to 10.5 percent. Second, OTS upgraded the thrift's CAMELS[4] composite rating to 1. OTS also did not identify the thrift's improper use of interest reserves prior to its March 2009 examination. We referred the thrift's inappropriate use of interest reserves to the Treasury Inspector General's Office of Investigations.

We concluded that OTS used its authority under PCA in accordance with PCA requirements.

OTS conducted an internal failed bank review of First Bank of Idaho and, among other things, identified four areas of weakness in OTS's supervisory response to First Bank of Idaho's concentrations in higher-risk loan areas. Our MLR affirmed OTS's internal findings and the need for corrective action.

OTS concurred with our recommendations that it ensure (1) action is taken on its internal failed

---

[4] CAMELS is an acronym for performance rating components for financial institutions: Capital adequacy, Asset quality, Management administration, Earnings, Liquidity, and Sensitivity to market risk. Numerical values range from 1 to 5, with 1 being the best rating and 5 being the worst. Each institution is also assigned a composite rating based on an assessment of its overall condition and level of supervisory concern.

bank review of First Bank of Idaho and (2) examiners sufficiently consider a thrift's risk profile when deciding whether to allow the thrift to lower its internal capital targets and when determining the thrift's CAMELS ratings. In a written response, OTS stated that it had issued guidance on prudent CRE loan workouts in October 2009 to remind examiners to appropriately review CRE loans, including loans supported by interest reserves. **(OIG-10-036)**

American Sterling Bank of Sugar Creek, Missouri (closed April 17, 2009; estimated loss to the Deposit Insurance Fund, $41.9 million)

The causes of American Sterling Bank's (ASB) failure were (1) losses sustained by its mortgage banking operation and (2) ineffective management and inadequate board oversight. Among other things, ASB senior management engaged in a litany of improper accounting transactions starting in 2007 that masked the thrift's deteriorating financial condition. We referred these transactions to the Treasury Inspector General's Office of Investigations. The thrift's inaccurate financial reporting delayed OTS from taking required prompt corrective action as the thrift's capital was depleted.

OTS's supervision did not adequately address ASB's problems early enough to prevent a material loss to the Deposit Insurance Fund. OTS did not require ASB to scale back its mortgage banking operation even though the bank was experiencing continuous losses and high staff turnover. In addition, OTS did not enforce federal banking regulations or follow its own guidance requiring ASB to hold additional capital to mitigate its recourse exposure to sold loans. OTS also did not adequately review a

noncash capital contribution of a participation loan to ASB by its holding company.

OTS conducted an internal failed bank review of ASB's failure and found that the failure primarily resulted from (1) losses related to the thrift's significant mortgage banking operation and an excessive concentration in held-for-sale loans and (2) inadequate management and insufficient independence from the operations of American Sterling Corporation, the thrift's holding company. The review concluded that OTS should have (1) taken increasingly aggressive steps with ASB's management and board to scale back or at least minimize the scope of the institution's mortgage operation and (2) placed more emphasis on ensuring that supervision and administration of the thrift by its board and management were not subject to the dominating adverse influence of the chief executive officer and the management of the corporation. Our MLR affirmed OTS's internal findings and the need for earlier corrective action.

We also concluded that as ASB adjusted and re-filed its financial reports as required by OTS, OTS properly and promptly used its authority under PCA.

We recommended that OTS (1) ensure that action is taken on its internal failed bank review of ASB; (2) remind supervisory and examination staff of the importance of requiring thrifts to hold capital to mitigate their recourse exposure on sold loans; (3) remind supervisory and examination staff to scrutinize capital contributions made to thrifts, especially noncash capital contributions; and (4) ensure examiners take forceful action to mitigate losses whenever a thrift's line of business incurs losses that threaten the viability of the institution. OTS concurred with our recommendations and agreed to implement the recommended actions in a timely manner. In a written response, OTS noted that it issued new internal guidelines in May 2009 to ensure appropriate enforcement action and issued a memorandum to thrift chief executive officers in July 2009 to address asset and liability concentrations and related risk management practices. **(OIG-10-011)**

Recovery Act Audits

During this semiannual period, we issued two audit reports as part of our ongoing oversight of Treasury's more than $20 billion of non-IRS spending authority under the American Recovery and Reinvestment Act of 2009 (Recovery Act). The two reports issued during this period were part of government-wide reviews coordinated by the Recovery Accountability and Transparency Board.[5] We consider our Recovery Act oversight a high priority along with our mandated work.

Treasury Should Ensure That Assessments of Staffing, Qualifications, and Training Needs Are Based on Reliable Survey Data

The Recovery Act requires that the Recovery Accountability and Transparency Board determine whether there are sufficient qualified acquisition and grant personnel overseeing

---

[5] The Recovery Accountability and Transparency Board was created by the Recovery Act with two goals: (1) to provide transparency in relation to the use of Recovery Act-related funds, and (2) to prevent and detect fraud, waste, and mismanagement. In addition, the Board maintains the Recovery.gov website that presents data on how Recovery money is being distributed by federal agencies and how the funds are being used by the recipients. The Board is comprised of a Chairman appointed by the President and 12 Inspectors General, including the Treasury Inspector General.

Recovery Act funds and whether such personnel are adequately trained. To do so, the Board developed a survey instrument to obtain a benchmark of the current acquisitions and grants workforce and to capture projected workforce data over the next year. We asked Treasury's Senior Accountable Official to administer the survey to its non-IRS workforce responsible for Recovery Act acquisitions and grants.

We found that Treasury's survey results were unreliable for making critical judgments on the adequacy of its Recovery Act workforce. Treasury management assessed its current contracts and grants workforce as adequate, but survey responses did not support this assessment. Furthermore, the workforce within the Office of the Fiscal Assistant Secretary overseeing $20 billion (88 percent) of the estimated $22 billion in Recovery Act grants in lieu of tax credits programs were not required to complete the survey. As a result, we concluded that Treasury's process for ensuring the completeness and reasonableness of survey responses was insufficient.

To address workforce concerns, we recommended that Treasury (1) comprehensively assess the adequacy of staffing levels, qualifications, and training of personnel responsible for Recovery Act contracts and grants, including the payments in lieu of tax credit programs, and consider the impact that the Recovery Act workload has on other mission-critical activities and take action based on this assessment; and (2) ensure that adequate policies and procedures are in place to provide reliable and complete data. Treasury management concurred with our recommendations and took action to increase the Recovery Act team and re-administer the survey instrument. **(OIG-10-002)**

Improvement Is Needed in Treasury's Data Quality Reviews

The Recovery Act provides for an unprecedented level of accountability and transparency for tax dollars spent on economic recovery. Recipients of Recovery Act funds are required to provide a quarterly report on the use of those funds under section 1512 of the act. OMB guidance to agencies requires that they develop internal policies and procedures for reviewing recipient-reported data, and the Recovery Accountability and Transparency Board has requested that inspectors general audit their respective agency's data quality review process. Because of the size of Treasury's grants-in-lieu-of-tax-credit Recovery Act programs for specified energy property and low-income housing and because recipients under these programs are required to report section 1512-like data to Treasury, we included the Office of the Fiscal Assistant Secretary, which administers the programs, in the scope of our work.

We found that while the office has a process for reviewing project performance reports under the low-income housing program, it had no system in place for collecting recipient data under the specified energy property program. We also noted that Treasury needed to establish written procedures for department wide oversight of data quality reviews and the need for the CDFI Fund to strengthen its recipient data quality reviews.

Treasury management agreed with our recommendations to (1) ensure the Office of the Fiscal Assistant Secretary establishes a system for recipients under the specified energy property program to submit annual project performance reports; (2) establish written policies and procedures for agency-wide

oversight of the data quality reviews; and (3) ensure that the CDFI Fund amend its existing policies and procedures to include steps to identify the proper source documents to review and procedures to be applied so that reviews are conducted consistently. **(OIG-10-034)**

Other Performance Audits

Suspicious Activity Report Data Quality Requires FinCEN's Continued Attention

One of FinCEN's critical functions under BSA is the collection, maintenance, and dissemination of data on suspicious financial transactions. These data are collected through suspicious activity reports (SAR) filed by financial institutions, including depository institutions, money services businesses, casinos and card clubs, and securities and futures firms. IRS, through its Enterprise Computing Center in Detroit, Michigan, serves as the government's central repository for BSA data. IRS maintains the information technology infrastructure and operations needed to process SAR data and convert the information to standardized electronic records for use by law enforcement and regulatory agencies. Our office has issued three prior audit reports on SAR data quality[6]. Each reported that a large percentage of SARs contained missing or inaccurate data.

Our latest audit concluded that SAR data quality had not significantly improved by 2006. We found that 59 percent of the approximately

---

6 FinCEN: *Heightened Management Attention Needed Over Longstanding SAR Data Quality Problems*, OIG-05-033 (Mar. 23, 2005); FinCEN: *Reliability of Suspicious Activity Reports*, OIG-03-035 (Dec. 18, 2002); *The Financial Crimes Enforcement Network Suspicious Activity Reporting System*, OIG-99-032 (Jan. 25, 1999).

1.1 million SARs filed in fiscal year 2006 contained omissions or incorrect, inconsistent, or inappropriate information in 1 or more of 17 data fields that FinCEN deemed critical to law enforcement. SARs filed by money services businesses had the highest percentage of data quality problems (88 percent), followed by SARs filed by securities and futures firms (50 percent), casinos and card clubs (49 percent), and depository institutions (34 percent). The critical fields that most often had missing or erroneous data were related to the subject's taxpayer identification number, address, and name.

The manner in which many SARs were completed suggests that the filers should have used more due diligence in preparing the submissions. Some of the missing data that we believe should have been available to the filer are the type of suspicious activity, the institution's address, and the location of the suspicious activity.

SAR data quality problems diminish the usefulness of the data for FinCEN, law enforcement, and other users. We also found disparities among similar institutions in the percentage of SARs they submitted with missing or erroneous data. These disparities raise the question of why certain institutions are consistently able to submit a higher percentage of complete and accurate SARs than others.

In addition, we found that system controls over the loading and processing of SAR data needed improvement. The control weaknesses prevented thousands of SARs with errors and other data quality problems from being identified and corrected during SAR processing. They affected the quality of the SAR data and in some cases the availability of the information to law enforcement. FinCEN management was

aware of some of the control issues identified by our audit and was working to correct the deficiencies. IRS officials stated that they were working with FinCEN to correct the problems related to the processing of BSA data.

We recommended that FinCEN (1) continue and enhance its filer education and outreach programs; (2) identify and refer to federal regulators those financial institutions with significant and recurring SAR quality problems; (3) coordinate with IRS to evaluate, implement, and improve controls over SAR data; and (4) request that IRS periodically notify FinCEN of SARs containing significant errors or missing critical data fields.

In a written response, FinCEN noted that the findings in the report were based on SAR data filed in fiscal year 2006 and that FinCEN has since completed efforts to improve the quality and integrity of SAR data. FinCEN concurred with our recommendations and noted that it has issued specific guidance to enhance filer education, established an initiative to identify systemic filing errors, and worked with federal regulators to resolve many of those types of errors. FinCEN also stated that it has worked with IRS to resolve matters associated with recording, processing, accounting for, and loading SARs. As part of its corrective action, FinCEN planned to have a SAR validation process in place to identify all SAR filings with significant errors for its compliance staff to monitor. FinCEN also planned to launch a program to modernize BSA information management, analysis, and dissemination. **(OIG-10-030)**

Bureau of Public Debt's Administrative Resource Center Processing of Personnel Actions for the CDFI Fund

During an audit of the procurement process that the CDFI Fund used for its information technology development and support contracts, we noted several issues with the Bureau of Public Debt's Administrative Resource Center (ARC) processing of the Fund's personnel actions. We did not conduct an audit of ARC's processing of personnel actions, but we consider these matters serious enough to warrant corrective action by management.

Specifically, we found that ARC processed a noncompetitive promotion for a CDFI Fund employee without obtaining all appropriate documentation from the Fund. ARC also did not properly maintain adequate records for the processed personnel action.

To address these matters, we recommended that the ARC take actions to obtain required documentation from clients, maintain complete position descriptions in HR Connect, Treasury's human resource processing system, and ensure that official personnel records are properly maintained. ARC concurred with our findings and implemented corrective actions.
(OIG-CA-10-005)

Significant Investigations

BPD Annuitant Theft Investigation

On May 19, 2009, our office was contacted by the Office of D.C. Pensions regarding the suspected theft of annuity payments to a deceased retired Metropolitan D.C. police officer. More specifically, the pension office continued to electronically deposit annuity payments into the annuitant's bank account after the retired officer's death in July 2005. Subsequently, approximately $54,000 in pension funds went into the account and was withdrawn.

It has been determined the annuitant's daughter was responsible for unlawfully receiving the benefits. Consequently, BPD and the Office of D.C. Pensions are in the process of reclaiming the funds. The U.S. Attorney's Office for the District of Columbia declined criminal prosecution in the matter.

Unauthorized Use of Government Credit Card by BEP Employee

Our office completed an investigation regarding a BEP employee who misused a government-issued credit card while on official travel. During our investigation, the employee admitted charging unauthorized expenses totaling approximately $7,500 to the card. The employee paid the balance of the charges incurred for the unauthorized expenses and subsequently resigned prior to the issuance of any disciplinary action.

Improper Acceptance of Gifts by a Treasury Official

We initiated an investigation of possible ethical violations by a senior official of Treasury's Office of Environmental Safety and Health. It was alleged that the senior official was allowed to attend a conference without paying the required conference registration fee on two occasions. The investigation confirmed the allegation. The senior official claimed to be unaware of the Treasury regulations which require an employee to obtain permission to attend the conference without paying the required fees. The results of the investigation have been sent to Departmental Offices for administrative remedies.

Abuse of Official Government Position by an FMS Official

We completed an investigation concerning allegations that an FMS senior official used public office for private gain. Specifically, it was alleged the official solicited numerous FMS employees to attend a professional conference in which the senior official received personal compensation for presenting at the conference.

Our investigation determined the FMS official violated both criminal law and Treasury policy by soliciting and approving training requisitions and utilizing government funds to register FMS employees for the conference. The U.S. Attorney's Office for the District of Maryland declined criminal prosecution of the senior official; therefore, the matter has since been referred to FMS for administrative remedies.

Abuse of Official Government Position by U.S. Mint Official

We received information from the Mint alleging that a senior Mint official misused his official position. Specifically, it was alleged that the official circumvented the terms and conditions of a Mint Penny Exchange Program by soliciting other Mint employees to purchase coins on his behalf, thus exceeding the maximum allowable coin purchase for an individual.

Our investigation revealed that the Mint official misused his position as a senior executive by requesting subordinate employees to perform actions outside of their job description on his behalf. We also determined that statements given by the Mint official during the investigation were untruthful and misleading. Subsequently, the matter was presented to the U.S. Attorney's Office for criminal prosecution, but prosecution was declined in lieu of administrative remedies against the official.

In October 2009, we forwarded the results of this matter to the Mint. As a result, the official received a letter of reprimand and was ordered to return the improperly obtained coins.

The following are updates to significant investigative activities reported in prior semiannual reports.

Sentencing in Postal Theft Conspiracy Targeting Treasury Checks

As previously reported, 13 subjects were indicted on June 19, 2008, for federal mail fraud, aiding and abetting, and forgery violations stemming from a scheme to steal numerous Treasury checks worth over $100,000 from the U.S. mail in Baltimore, Maryland.

Update

- On October 23, 2009, Tandria Boyd was sentenced to 30 months in prison followed by 3 years of supervised release for conspiracy to commit mail fraud, forged endorsement on a Treasury check, and aggravated identity theft. Boyd was also ordered to pay restitution in the amount of $10,000.

- On October 23, 2009, Chamarko Amin was sentenced to 48 months in prison, followed by 3 years of supervised release, on charges of conspiracy to commit mail fraud and aggravated identity theft. Amin was also ordered to pay restitution in the amount of $104,446.

- On October 30, 2009, David Cooley was sentenced to 65 months in prison followed by 3 years of supervised release for conspiracy to commit mail fraud and aggravated identity theft. Cooley was also ordered to pay restitution in the amount of $104,446.

- On January 7, 2010, Leonard Jenkins was sentenced to 3 years in prison followed by 3 years of supervised release for mail fraud, theft of mail, and aggravated identity theft. Jenkins was also ordered to pay restitution in the amount of $104,446.

Management Implication Reports Issued

During the reporting period, we issued management implication reports (MIR) summarizing systemic vulnerabilities that we observed related to the Mint's Mutilated Coin Exchange Program and the BEP Mutilated Currency Exchange Program.

Report on Mint's Mutilated Coin Program

In 1911, Treasury established a program to allow people and businesses to exchange coins that were damaged by flood, fire, or other means and therefore not acceptable as legal tender. In recent years, the Mint has observed a significant increase in the number and quantity of mutilated coins being submitted for redemption.

The increase in mutilated coin submissions has raised concern by the Mint and led to inquiries of various entities redeeming coins about the source of the coins. The Mint's concerns centered on the value and frequency of mutilated coin redemptions by a relatively small number of individuals and corporations.

Our subsequent investigation revealed several weaknesses that, if addressed, would likely improve the integrity of the Mutilated Coin Program. As such, we submitted the completed MIR to Mint management addressing the vulnerabilities of the program.

Report on BEP's Mutilated Currency Exchange Program

In the late 1800s, the U.S. government enacted legislation requiring Treasury to exchange damaged or mutilated U.S. currency on a one-for-one basis. This allowed the public to exchange currency that, due to its condition, might not otherwise be accepted as legal tender. This program, known as the Mutilated Currency Exchange Program, is administered by BEP. BEP maintains a professional staff of forensic experts who examine each note that is submitted for exchange to determine its authenticity before redeeming it.

In January 2007, BEP management contacted our office and requested assistance after noting a series of requests for large-value currency redemptions that appeared suspicious.

We have participated in several joint investigations with the U.S. Secret Service and U.S. Immigration and Customs Enforcement, which have the authority to affect asset seizure and forfeiture, in investigations involving redemption of intentionally mutilated currency. To date, these investigations have led to many significant seizures by other federal agencies.

These investigations revealed numerous deficiencies in the Mutilated Currency Exchange Program. Subsequently, we submitted a MIR to BEP to assist in correcting the weaknesses identified.

Other OIG Accomplishments and Activity

CIGIE Award Ceremony

At the Annual Council of the Inspectors General on Integrity and Efficiency Ceremony held on October 20, 2009, Treasury OIG received a prestigious Audit Award for Excellence in recognition of its MLR review of IndyMac Bank, FSB. IndyMac's failure resulted in an estimated loss of $10.7 billion to FDIC's Deposit Insurance Fund, the most costly failure to trigger an MLR review of the current economic crisis.

IndyMac MLR team members Don Benson, Audit Director; Maryann Costello, Auditor-in-Charge; Sharon Torosian, Audit Manager; and Jeanne Degagne. Not pictured are Tim Cargell, Auditor-in-Charge; Jason Madden, Auditor; Cynthia Milanez, Referencer; John Colantoni, Senior Audit Specialist, FDIC OIG; and Titus Simmons, Senior Audit Specialist, FDIC OIG.

Efforts Made by Inspectors General to Raise the MLR Threshold

As discussed in our last semiannual report, in January 2009 Inspector General Thorson and the Inspectors General of FDIC and the Federal Reserve System sent letters to the Congress asking for consideration to raise the current threshold for MLRs for failed banks of $25 million, established in 1991, to between $300 million and $500 million. The request was made so that resources could be made available for other work. Additionally, in May 2009, the same three Inspectors General testified before the Subcommittee on Oversight and Investigations of the House Committee on Financial Services on that issue.

In his testimony, Mr. Thorson stressed the importance of MLRs and described the impact of the unprecedented number of MLRs during the current financial crisis on our office's ability to do other important oversight work.

In July 2009, the House passed H.R. 3330, Improved Oversight by Financial Inspectors General Act of 2009, which would, among other things, raise the threshold loss for MLRs to $200 million. On April 15, 2010, S. 3217, the Restoring American Financial Stability Act of 2010, was introduced in the Senate. Section 987 of that legislation includes a provision to establish the MLR threshold for failed banks at (1) $100 million from September 30, 2009, through December 31, 2010; (2) $75 million for 2011; and (3) $50 million for 2012 and beyond. Like H.R. 3330, the Senate bill would require some level of review by the cognizant OIG of all bank failures.

Our office continues to believe the MLR threshold should be raised.

The Recovery Accountability and Transparency Board Activity

The Recovery Accountability and Transparency Board (the Board) was established by the Recovery Act to coordinate and conduct oversight of Recovery Act funds for purposes of preventing and detecting fraud, waste, and mismanagement. Additionally, the Board provides an unprecedented level of transparency and accountability in relation to the use of Recovery-related funds.

The Board is comprised of 12 Inspectors General, from the 12 federal agencies charged with awarding and distributing the largest amounts of Recovery Act funds. Treasury Inspector General Thorson serves on the Board.

Among other things, to meet its objectives, the Board coordinates broad oversight audits and reviews of Recovery Act functions and activities throughout the federal government. This is accomplished primarily with the assistance of Inspectors General who serve on the Board. The Board issues quarterly and annual reports to the President and Congress and, if necessary, "flash reports" on matters that require immediate attention.

The Board also maintains the Recovery.gov website so the American people can see how Recovery money is being distributed by federal agencies and how the funds are being used by the recipients.

In addition to the Board itself there are several other committees and subgroups that support the Board's activities. One such subgroup is the Recovery Act Working Group which consists of representatives from 29 OIGs. Our Deputy Inspector General, Dennis Schindel is a full time member of the working Group.

External Peer Review of the Treasury OIG Office of Audit Resulted in a Pass Rating

Audit organizations that perform audits and attestation engagements of federal government programs and operations are required by

Government Auditing Standards to undergo an external peer review every 3 years. The objective of an external peer review is to determine whether, during the period under review, the audit organization's system of quality control was suitably designed and whether the audit organization was complying with its quality control system in order to provide the audit organization with reasonable assurance of conforming to applicable professional standards.

During this semiannual period, the Department of State OIG completed an external peer of the Treasury OIG audit organization and rendered a *pass* rating, the highest rating attainable, for the year ended March 31, 2009. In a report dated November 19, 2009, the Department of State also noted two findings with our system of audit quality control for which we are taking corrective action. The external peer review report is available on our website.

OIG Audit Leadership Roles

Treasury OIG's audit professionals actively support and serve on various important public and private professional organizations supporting the federal audit community. Examples of Treasury OIG Audit personnel participation in these organizations follow:

Joel Grover, Deputy Assistant Inspector General for Financial Management and Information Technology Audits, serves as co-chair of the Federal Audit Executive Council Financial Statements Committee and is actively involved in developing and coordinating the Council's positions on a variety of accounting and auditing issues related to federal financial reporting. The committee also jointly sponsors with GAO an annual federal financial statement audit update conference.

Mr. Grover is also a member of the Government Performance and Accountability Committee of the American Institute of Certified Public Accountants. The mission of this Committee is to (1) promote greater government accountability and integrity of government operations, information and information systems; (2) promote and encourage increased participation and involvement by certified public accountants (CPA) in government within the Institute; (3) enhance the professional image and value of CPAs in government; (4) provide advice and counsel to the Institute on the needs of CPAs in government, and (5) serve as a conduit for communications among CPAs in government, the Institute, and other professional organizations.

Mr. Grover serves as a co-chair of the Maryland Association of Certified Public Accountants Members in Government Committee. Among other activities, the Committee sponsors an annual training conference on government/not-for-profit accounting and auditing issues.

Bob Taylor, Deputy Assistant Inspector General for Performance Audits, **Kieu Rubb**, Audit Director, and **Cedric Hammond**, Manager, served as facilitators for a training course on the Council of the Inspectors General on Integrity and Efficiency Audit Committee's external peer review guide. The day long training was held during March 2010 at the FDIC Seidman Center in Arlington, Virginia.

OIG Special Agent Recognized by United States Attorney for Investigative Efforts

On January 21, 2010, **Special Agent Jason Metrick** received a recognition award from the U.S. Attorney for the District of Maryland, Rod J. Rosenstein. The award was given to Agent Metrick for his outstanding contributions to criminal investigations and prosecutions in Maryland related to identity theft, including the case of United States v. Amin. During the Amin investigation, 12 defendants were convicted for their participation in a scheme to steal and negotiate Treasury checks totaling more than $100,000. The defendants all received prison sentences, ranging from 24 to 75 months.

Referenced in this picture are agents from Treasury, U.S. Secret Service, Department of Transportation OIG, U.S. Postal Service OIG, U.S. Postal Inspection Service, District of Columbia OIG, the U.S. Attorney's Office for the District of Columbia, and Rod J. Rosenstein, U.S. Attorney for the District of Maryland.

Treasury Team Wins a 2009 Presidential Energy Management Award

Zenobia Ziegler, an Office of Investigations Program Analyst, was part of the Department of the Treasury Energy and Transportation Management Team whose efforts led to significant reductions of energy use by fleet managers across the Department. In recognition, the team was awarded a 2009 Presidential Energy Management Award.

The Presidential Awards for Leadership in Federal Energy Management recognize federal employees for their support, leadership, and efforts in promoting and improving federal energy management.

U.S. Immigration and Customs Enforcement Partnership Award Presented to Office of Investigations

On February 19, 2010, the Office of Investigations received the Immigration and Customs Enforcement Partnership Award. The award was given to the Office of Investigations in recognition of its work on an investigation of abuse of the BEP Mutilated Currency Exchange Program by individuals who submitted intentionally mutilated U.S. currency for reimbursement. The investigation resulted in a significant seizure of U.S. currency by the U.S. Attorney's Office.

Pictured from left to right are James Dinkins, Director of the Office of Investigations, Immigration and Customs Enforcement; James Howell, Special Agent, Treasury OIG; John Phillips, Special Agent-in-Charge Treasury OIG; Richard Hattauer, BEP; and John Torres, Special Agent-in-Charge, Immigration and Customs Enforcement..

Increase in OIG Workforce

OIG has continued to aggressively recruit and hire staff to meet the increasing workload associated primarily with financial institution failures, but also to meet oversight responsibilities for Recovery Act programs administered by Treasury. Since the beginning of fiscal year 2010, through March 31, 2010, OIG has added 37 staff, with an additional 6 selected and in the pipeline.

OIG Receives Combined Federal Campaign Chairman's Award

During Treasury's 2009 Combined Federal Campaign closing ceremony on February 25, 2010, hosted by the Assistant Secretary for Management, Dan Tangherlini, OIG was one of several bureaus presented with the Chairman's Award for exceeding both dollar and participation goals. The OIG campaign coordinator, Jay Koehler, accepted the award for OIG.

Statistical Summary

Summary of OIG Activity

For the 6 months ended March 31, 2010

OIG Activity	Number or Dollar Value
Office of Counsel Activity	
Regulation and legislation reviews	2
Instances where information was refused	0
Office of Audit Activities	
Reports issued (audits and evaluations)	40
Disputed audit recommendations	0
Significant revised management decisions	0
Management decision in which the IG disagrees	0
Monetary benefits (audit)	
Questioned costs	0
Funds put to better use	0
Revenue enhancements	0
Total monetary benefits	$0
Office of Investigations Activities	
Criminal and judicial actions (including joint investigations)	
Cases referred for prosecution and/or litigation	6
Cases accepted for prosecution and/or litigation	0
Arrests	0
Indictments/informations	0
Convictions (by trial and plea)	0

Significant Unimplemented Recommendations

For reports issued prior to April 1, 2009

The following list of OIG audit reports with unimplemented recommendations is based on information in Treasury's automated audit recommendation tracking system, which is maintained by Treasury management officials.

Number	Date	Report Title and Recommendation Summary
OIG-06-030	05/06	*Terrorist Financing/Money Laundering: FinCEN Has Taken Steps to Better Analyze Bank Secrecy Act Data but Challenges Remain* FinCEN should enhance the current FinCEN database system or acquire a new system. An improved system should provide for complete and accurate information on the case type, status, resources, and time expended in

performing the analysis. This system should also have the proper security controls to maintain integrity of the data. (1 recommendation)

OIG-08-008   11/07   *Management Letter for Fiscal Year 2007 Audit of the Federal Financing Bank's Financial Statements*
The Federal Financing Bank should follow through with its plan to upgrade the Loan Management and Control System Database Management System to a supported version of Oracle. (1 recommendation)

OIG-08-018   12/07   *Management Letter for the Fiscal Year 2007 Audit of the United States Mint's Financial Statements*
The Mint should establish and implement policies and procedures for the retirement of assets to ensure that Excess Property forms are properly completed, filed, and available for examination for a reasonable time period after the retirement transaction. (1 recommendation)

OIG-08-035   06/08   *Network Security at the Office of the Comptroller of the Currency Needs Improvement*
OCC should ensure that the principle of least privilege is enforced and applied to all OCC computer users as required by OCC policy. (1 recommendation)

OIG-08-036   06/08   *BEP Needs to Enforce and Strengthen Controls on Its Eastern Currency Facility to Prevent and Detect Employee Theft*
BEP management should (1) establish clear, written policies and procedures that specify assignment of responsibility and actions to be taken when discrepancies are found in the production process and (2) ensure that employees, including supervisors, are trained and periodically retrained in product security-related policies and procedures. (2 recommendations)

OIG-08-046   09/08   *Federal Information Security Management Act Fiscal Year 2008 Performance Audit*
OTS should continue with bureau plans to resolve the security weaknesses identified during the certification and accreditation process by the end of the interim authorization period, December 31, 2008, and achieve a full authority to operate during the fiscal year 2009 FISMA reporting period. (1 recommendation)

OIG-09-006   11/08   *Audit of the Department of the Treasury's Fiscal Years 2008 and 2007 Financial Statements*

The Assistant Secretary for Management and Chief Financial Officer and the Deputy Assistant Secretary for Human Resources and Chief Human Capital Officer, with input from the Director of Accounting and Internal Controls, as appropriate, document policy and procedures related to Federal Credit Reform Act transactions, periodically examine performance of the credit programs to re-estimate cash flow projections and assumptions, and have affected personnel continue to consult with other Federal agencies that have substantial credit reform accounting experience. (1 recommendation)

OIG-09-009   11/08   *The Department of the Treasury's Special-Purpose Financial Statements for Fiscal Years 2008 and 2007*

The Department should improve controls to ensure that the special-purpose financial statement and accompanying notes are accurately prepared in accordance with the instructions contained in Chapter 4700. Internal control improvements should include appropriate supervisory review, by responsible officials of the closing package prior to lock down.
(1 recommendation)

OIG-09-013   12/08   *Safety and Soundness: Material Loss Review of ANB Financial, NA*

OCC should reassess their guidance and examination procedures in the Comptroller's Handbook related to bank use of wholesale funding with a focus on heavy reliance on brokered deposits and other non-retail deposit funding sources for growth. (1 recommendation)

OIG-09-014   1/09   *Information Technology: United States Department of the Treasury's Compliance with Section 522 of the Consolidated Appropriations Act of 2005*

The Office of Privacy and Treasury Records management should (1) prepare a report to Congress on an annual basis on activities of the Treasury that affect privacy, including complaints of privacy violations; implementation of Section 552a of Title 5, 11 United States Code; internal controls; and other relevant matters; and (2) record a formal written report on the use of information in an identifiable form, as well as privacy and data protection policies and procedures with the OIG. (2 recommendations)

OIG-09-016   1/09   *Management Letter for Fiscal Year 2008 Audit of the United States Mint's Financial Statements*

The Mint should (1) update policies and procedures for the retirement of assets to ensure that retirement forms are completed for all assets retired and that the forms are retained for examination for a reasonable time period after the retirement transaction., (2) ensure that all assets with barcodes are scanned as part of the inventory or documented as a reconciling item with an explanation of the circumstances, and (3) implement an inventory standard operating procedure for Numismatic Inventory.
(3 recommendations)

OIG-09-024   1/09   *General Management: Treasury Should Reactivate State-Held Federal Unclaimed Assets Recovery Program (Corrective Action Verification on OIG-02-105)*

Treasury should reactivate the state-held federal unclaimed assets recovery program with appropriate policies, procedures, and controls. This recommendation has a potential revenue enhancement monetary benefit of $10.5 million. (1 recommendation)

OIG-09-027   1/09   *Management Letter for Fiscal Year 2008 Audit of the Office of the Comptroller of the Currency's Financial Statements*

OCC should continue to dedicate resources to fully implement the necessary System Management Server process automatically and promptly detect and remove unauthorized personal and public domain software from OCC systems (workstations) and implement controls to restrict users from downloading and installing unapproved software. (1 recommendation)

Summary of Instances Where Information Was Refused

October 1, 2009, through March 31, 2010

There were no such instances during this period.

Listing of Audit and Evaluation Reports Issued

October 1, 2009, through March 31, 2010

Financial Audits and Attestation Engagement

Audit of the United States Mint's Schedule of Custodial Deep Storage Gold and Silver Reserves as of September 30, 2009 and 2008, OIG-10-003, 10/21/09

Audit of Bureau of Engraving and Printing's Fiscal Years 2009 and 2008 Financial Statements, OIG-10-004, 11/4/09

Financial Management's Report on the Bureau of the Public Debt Trust Fund Management Branch Schedules for Selected Trust Funds as of and for the Year Ended September 30, 2009, OIG-10-005, 11/6/09

Management Letter for Fiscal Year 2009 Audit of Bureau of Engraving and Printing's Financial Statements, OIG-10-006, 11/10/09

Audit of the Federal Financing Bank's Fiscal Years 2009 and 2008 Financial Statements, OIG-10-007, 11/12/09

Management Letter for Fiscal Year 2009 Audit of the Federal Financing Bank's Financial Statements, OIG-10-008, 11/12/09

Audit of the Community Development Financial Institutions Fund's Fiscal Year 2009 Financial Statements and Fiscal Year 2008 Statement of Financial Position, OIG-10-009, 11/16/09

Management Letter for Fiscal Year 2009 Audit of the Community Development Financial Institutions Fund's Financial Statements, OIG-10-010, 11/16/09

Audit of the Department of the Treasury Forfeiture Fund's Fiscal Years 2009 and 2008 Financial Statements, OIG-10-012, 11/24/09

Audit of the United States Mint's Fiscal Years 2009 and 2008 Financial Statements, OIG-10-013, 12/1/09

Management Letter for Fiscal Year 2009 Audit of the United States Mint's Financial Statements, OIG-10-014, 2/1/09

Audit of the Office of D.C. Pensions' Fiscal Years 2009 and 2008 Financial Statements, OIG-10-015, 12/7/09

Management Letter for Fiscal Year 2009 Audit of the Office of D.C. Pensions' Financial Statements, OIG-10-016, 12/7/09

Audit of the Financial Management Service's Fiscal Years 2009 and 2008 Schedules of Non-Entity Government-Wide Cash, OIG-10-018, 12/9/09

Audit of the Financial Management Service's Fiscal Years 2009 and 2008 Schedules of Non-Entity Assets, Non-Entity Costs and Custodial Revenue, OIG-10-019, 12/9/09

Management Report For Fiscal Year 2009 Audit of the Financial Management Service's Schedule of Non-Entity Assets, Non-Entity Costs and Custodial Revenue (Sensitive But Unclassified), OIG-10-020, 12/10/09

Management Letter for Fiscal Year 2009 Audit of the Financial Management Service's Schedule of Non-Entity Government-wide Cash, OIG-10-021, 12/10/09

Management Report for Fiscal Year 2009 Audit of the Financial Management Service's Schedule of Non-Entity Government-wide Cash, (Sensitive But Unclassified), OIG-10-022, 12/10/09

Audit of the Department of Treasury's Fiscal Years 2009 and 2008 Financial Statements, OIG-10-023, 12/16/09

Audit of the Office of the Comptroller of the Currency's Fiscal Years 2009 and 2008 Financial Statements, OIG-10-024, 12/22/09

Management Letter for Fiscal Year 2009 Audit of the Office of the Comptroller of the Currency's Financial Statements, OIG-10-025, 12/22/09

Audit of the Financial Crimes Enforcement Network's Fiscal Years 2009 and 2008 Financial Statements, OIG-10-026, 12/22/09

Audit of the Exchange Stabilization Fund's Fiscal Years 2009 and 2008 Financial Statements, OIG-10-027, 12/22/09

Management Letter for Fiscal Year 2009 Audit of the Exchange Stabilization Fund's Financial Statements, OIG-10-028, 12/22/09

Audit of the Department of the Treasury's Special-Purpose Financial Statements for Fiscal Years 2009 and 2008, OIG-10-029, 1/7/10

Audit of the Office of Thrift Supervision's Fiscal Years 2009 and 2008 Financial Statements, OIG-10-031, 1/19/10

Management Letter for Fiscal Year 2009 Audit of the Office of Thrift Supervision's Financial Statements, OIG-10-032, 1/19/10

Management Letter for Fiscal Year 2009 Audit of the Department of the Treasury's Financial Statements, OIG-10-035, 2/4/10

Information Technology Audits and Evaluations

Information Technology: Improvements Needed in CDFI Fund's Access Controls and Configuration Management, OIG-10-037, 2/25/10

Information Technology: The Department of Treasury Federal Information Security Management Act Fiscal Year 2009 Evaluation, OIG-CA-10-003, 11/13/09

Performance Audits

Safety and Soundness: Material Loss Review of TeamBank, National Association, OIG-10-001, 10/7/09

Recovery Act: Treasury Should Ensure That Assessments of Staffing, Qualifications, and Training Needs Are Based on Reliable Survey Data, OIG-10-002, 10/13/09

Safety and Soundness: Material Loss Review of American Sterling Bank, OIG-10-011, 11/25/09

Safety and Soundness: Material Loss Review of Omni National Bank, OIG-10-017, 12/9/09

SAR Data Quality Requires FinCEN's Continued Attention, OIG-10-030, 1/19/10

Safety and Soundness: Material Loss Review of Silverton Bank, N.A., OIG-10-033, 1/22/10

Recovery Act: Improvement Is Needed in Treasury's Data Quality Reviews, OIG-10-034, 1/28/10

Safety and Soundness: Material Loss Review of First Bank of Idaho, OIG-10-036, 2/16/10

Safety and Soundness: Material Loss Review of Citizens National Bank, OIG-10-038, 3/22/10

General Management: Administrative Resource Center Processing of Personnel Actions for the Community Development Financial Institution Fund, OIG-CA-10-005, 2/1/10

Audit Reports Issued With Questioned Costs

October 1, 2009, through March 31, 2010

Category	Total No. of Reports	Total Questioned Costs[a]	Total Unsupported Costs[a]
For which no management decision had been made by beginning of reporting period[b]	1	$995,367	0
Which were issued during the reporting period	0	0	0
Subtotals	1	$995,367	0
For which a management decision was made during the reporting period	0	0	0
Dollar value of disallowed costs	0	0	0
Dollar value of costs not disallowed	0	0	0
For which no management decision was made by the end of the reporting period	1	$995,367	0
For which no management decision was made within 6 months of issuance	1	$995,367	0

[a] Questioned costs include unsupported costs.
[b] Audit was performed by the Defense Contract Audit Agency.

Audit Reports Issued With Recommendations That Funds Be Put to Better Use

October 1, 2009, through March 31, 2010

At the beginning of the period, there were no audit reports from prior periods pending a management decision on recommendations that funds be put to better use. There were also no audit reports issued during this period with recommendations that funds be put to better use.

Previously Issued Audit Reports Pending Management Decisions (Over 6 Months)

We have one previously issued audit report pending a management decision: Contract Audit: Spectra Systems Corporation's Cost Proposal in Response to Solicitation TEP-09-007, OIG-09-040A, dated July 15, 2009, with $995,367 in questioned costs. We are working with BEP management to resolve this matter.

Significant Revised Management Decisions

October 1, 2009, through March 31, 2010

There were no significant revised management decisions during the period.

Significant Disagreed Management Decisions

October 1, 2009, through March 31, 2010

There were no management decisions this period with which the IG was in disagreement.

References to the Inspector General Act

	Requirement	Page
Section 4(a)(2)	Review of legislation and regulations	28
Section 5(a)(1)	Significant problems, abuses, and deficiencies	5-23
Section 5(a)(2)	Recommendations with respect to significant problems, abuses, and deficiencies	5-23
Section 5(a)(3)	Significant unimplemented recommendations described in previous semiannual reports	28-31
Section 5(a)(4)	Matters referred to prosecutive authorities	28
Section 5(a)(5)	Summary of instances where information was refused	32
Section 5(a)(6)	List of audit reports	32-34
Section 5(a)(7)	Summary of significant reports	5-23
Section 5(a)(8)	Audit reports with questioned costs	35
Section 5(a)(9)	Recommendations that funds be put to better use	35
Section 5(a)(10)	Summary of audit reports issued before the beginning of the reporting period for which no management decision had been made	35-36
Section 5(a)(11)	Significant revised management decisions made during the reporting period	35
Section 5(a)(12)	Management decisions with which the IG is in disagreement	36
Section 5(a)(13)	Instances of unresolved FFMIA noncompliance	8
Section 5(d)	Serious or flagrant problems, abuses, or deficiencies	N/A
Section 6(b)(2)	Report to Secretary when information or assistance is unreasonably refused	N/A

Abbreviations

ARC	Administrative Resource Center
ASB	American Sterling Bank
BEP	Bureau of Engraving and Printing
BPD	Bureau of the Public Debt
BSA	Bank Secrecy Act
CMO	collateralized mortgage obligations
CNB	Citizens National Bank
CPA	certified public accountant
CPP	Capital Purchase Program
CRE	commercial real estate
EESA	Emergency Economic Stabilization Act
FDIC	Federal Deposit Insurance Corporation
FDICIA	Federal Deposit Insurance Corporation Improvement Act
FinCEN	Financial Crimes Enforcement Network
FISMA	Federal Information Security Management Act
FMS	Financial Management Service
GAO	Government Accountability Office
IRS	Internal Revenue Service
MIR	Management Implication Reports
MLR	material loss review
OCC	Office of the Comptroller of the Currency
OFAC	Office of Foreign Assets Control
OIG	Office of Inspector General
OMB	Office of Management and Budget
OTS	Office of Thrift Supervision
PCA	Prompt Corrective Action
SAR	suspicious activity reports
TARP	Troubled Asset Relief Program
TIER	Treasury Information Executive Repository

Eric M. Thorson, Treasury Inspector General

Eric Thorson was sworn into office on August 12, 2008, as the Treasury Inspector General. Before joining Treasury, Mr. Thorson served as the Inspector General for the Small Business Administration.